Burrows and Colton

The Art of Retouching

Thrid American Edition

Burrows and Colton

The Art of Retouching
Thrid American Edition

ISBN/EAN: 9783337002749

Printed in Europe, USA, Canada, Australia, Japan

Cover: Foto ©Thomas Meinert / pixelio.de

More available books at **www.hansebooks.com**

ANTHONY'S PHOTO SERIES, No. 6.

THE

ART OF

RETOUCHING

BY

BURROWS & COLTON

THIRD AMERICAN EDITION

REVISED BY THE AUTHOR, J. P. OURDAN

NEW YORK:
E. & H. T. ANTHONY & CO.
1891.

891 _ 50 1729

PREFACE.

WHEN the "ART OF RETOUCHING" was first written, little hope was entertained that it would be so universally welcomed as it has been ; and as edition after edition was readily disposed of—copies finding their way to all parts of the world, with favorable reports from every quarter —the author decided to fully rewrite and enlarge the original book, introducing many useful points noted by him during his sojourn in America. Having retouched many negatives during that time he is able to make a more com plete and exhaustive treatise, embracing points applicable to American taste and negatives which would never occur in European practice,

adjusting instructive matter to the requirements
of both. The author still disclaims the idea of
encroaching upon others' work, though endeavor-
ing to lay before his readers a lucid quotation of
other professionals' experience as well as his own,
which is based upon some years of study in artistic pursuits, both in this country and abroad.
The same characteristic absence of elaboration
which gave the first edition of this book such a
reputation, distinguishes this one throughout; all
superfluous matter has been carefully avoided,
and everything contained in this edition is guar-
anteed to be perfectly practicable—can be demonstrated to anyone requiring it.

INTRODUCTION.

FOR the past few years, nearly every subject connected with Photography has been written up to such an extent that little remains to be said concerning it. Retouching seems to be the only one which has not received the attention it unquestionably deserves; for, as beautiful as the Art of Photography is, there can be no doubt that it abounds in shortcomings, and to meet these Retouching is without dispute a powerful adjunct.

Articles have appeared at different times which have treated generally of its effect and advantages, but none have given the reader an insight into the details of this interesting and important branch. The object of this book is to give such minute and detailed instructions, as to enable anyone with an ordinary amount of taste to acquire the art of Retouching in a short time. Of course it is not implied that one is to succeed in becoming a first-class retoucher in a few days by simply reading through the directions given. The production of these artistic effects cannot be learned mechanically. It would take one year of careful study to communicate to the work, the high and rare qualities of art, and when accomplished, the labor would scarcely be appreciated by the public generally as an individual acquirement, judging as it does of the finished picture as a whole. Retouching as an artistic pursuit, has not been carried to such a degree of excellence as to demand a high artistic feeling, though naturally the more of it one possesses the better work he will produce. While admitting that a few personal lessons at the hands of a practical retoucher with an art education, would greatly advance beginners, it is claimed that by following carefully the instructions given, for whichever system it is proposed to learn, results may be obtained with reasonably

short practice, which would take the learner
months to master by the ordinary course of pro-
cedure. One thing is particularly recommended,
i.e., to adhere to one system until mastered; for
by trying a little of this method and a little of another, an uncertain style is acquired, to practice
which, takes longer time than is necessary, from
the fact of there being no established order in the
routine employed, resulting in effects altogether
unsatisfactory. This book being intended as a
practical instructor, we will launch at once into the
subject, treating each point with that degree of
care and minuteness of description necessary to
give the reader a clear conception of it.

THE ART OF RETOUCHING.

CHAPTER I.

FOR the production of good work it is very necessary to be capable of determining at a glance just what amount of labor is required upon a negative, and what alterations are to be made to improve its printing qualities without destroying its character. This will take more or less practice, depending upon the retoucher's knowledge and artistic talent, it being impossible to apply the remedy if one does not possess the power of correctly appreciating a defect. As we remarked in the preface, the greater artistic talent one possesses, the easier he can portray in his mind a point deficient in physical resemblance or a possible improvement. All the niceties of execution are to a large extent mechanical, but the power of vivifying a portrait is an undeniable intellectual faculty. To render explanation more explicit, in the endeavor to show the reader the amount of work to be done upon a negative, figured plates are introduced which describe all the muscles and lines of a face. The reader is recommended to refer frequently to these while practicing, as they will materially assist him to model correctly, and accustom him to mentally dissect a face when commencing to retouch, a practice which will aid greatly in the student's advancement. Throughout this work the reader is assumed to be entirely ignorant of the Art of Retouching ; and although this may render the book a little insipid to some, to the beginner it is infinitely important to treat the subject thus, in order to give him all possible practical information. It will greatly assist any one taking up retouching as a vocation, if he will make a careful study of the anatomy of faces, and learn to give to or retain in each face, the peculiarity of character it pos-sesses. At the same time it is equally important to improve the printing qualities of the negative and to modify the lighting and expression; but to know how to do this, and, in so doing, to lose the points above mentioned would be useless.

The study of facial anatomy and analysis will by no means prove beneficial as applied to nega-tives only, but once mastered, it may be used as a groundwork for any future artistic study, such as crayon, oil, or India-ink and pastel work. In-deed it is to be regretted that many of the "Cray-on Artists" had not paid due attention to this branch; had they done so, crayon work would have enjoyed a wider popularity to-day; but the hundreds of vile productions that are circulated through lack of knowledge of the anatomy of the human face, owing to which likenesses are lost, have so condemned this kind of portraiture that the public have lost faith in it, regarding adher-ence to original likeness as a matter of chance.

These remarks are not altogether inapplicable to photography ; how comparatively few photographers can always ensure a truthful likeness ! Nothing can be more annoying than to produce a faultless negative (chemically and artistically) and have it ruined by the retoucher, who without any regard to expression, drawing or anatomy, aims simply at making the negative perfectly smooth and fine. He succeeds in this manner in effacing all traces of character, and as a rule treats faces of either sex, and all ages, in precisely the same way, instead of which he should have striven to retain the peculiarities he has removed, and not work the face of a man of sixty, as delicately as a schoolboy's.

Every individual is distinguished by certain peculiarities, and these must be so treated that where they exist prominently as defective individualities, they will remain, and yet not attract special attention.   As the student progresses, bearing in mind the hints advanced, he will soon attain proficiency in this.   He will learn to make with facility any alteration taste may suggest, such as a fixed, staring and unnatural look, assumed by so many persons while sitting for a portrait, into an easy, natural smile ; or to change the forced, sinister smirk assumed under like conditions into a calm and pleasing expression. The plates will be found of great service here ; as all muscular organisms are subject to the same lineal changes under parallel circumstances, such as grief, joy, pain, pleasure, etc., the plates may be adjusted to any portrait. These changes are all possible, and one unacquainted with the method of effecting them is often surprised at the power a retoucher has to alter a negative to suit his taste. This is in truth much easier upon negatives than in drawing or painting, particularly to those whose knowledge of drawing is limited, as in a negative the modelling of the face is all indicated, leaving the retoucher only photographic exaggerations to overcome, and to harmonize the whole so that each feature effectively maintains its place without importuning the spectator's eye. The most difficult subjects are the persons who insist upon being taken "*just as they are.*" Negatives of such may be flattered with impunity, as it usually turns out that they do not wish to be represented "*just as they are.*" When the indications of modelling are too weak to print, they can always be seen in a soft, transmitted light sufficiently to enable the retoucher to strengthen them to any extent. The common error into which beginners are very apt to fall, is a tendency to give too much rotundity to the face, producing prints absolutely devoid of character, there being a total absence of the delicate modulation and half tone which gives a picture all the life it may have.

Exaggerations of photography have also to be looked to. These are the most formidable difficulties it is the retoucher's misfortune to encounter. Perhaps the most troublesome of all, is the displacement (if such a term can be applied) of the nose. It is surprising the number of different shapes that may be given to this feature by the slightest alteration of the light or the position of

the sitter or camera. The artist photographer
builds much of his reputation upon a knowledge
of this fact—his conversance with the effects and
defects obtainable by such changes enabling him
to avoid the latter and avail himself of the bene-
fits of a judicious employment of the former.

As an instance of this, take the case of a lady
whose nose is of the *retroussé* stamp. Mr. Smith
photographs the subject, posing her with the head
slightly elevated and the camera raised to a level
with, or even a little lower than, the sitter's head,
and in such a position as to give a nearly full-face
portrait, the light reaching the sitter from the front
and top. As a natural consequence the patron is
not satisfied with her portrait. The shape of her
nose has been completely altered, the end enlarged
and the bridge flattened, giving the lady an expression quite foreign to her. Mr. Brown is the
next photographer visited, who, being an artist, de-
cides at once the position, etc., most suitable to this
feature, and accordingly gives his sitter an easy,
meditative and artistic pose, avoiding both full face

and profile, allowing a soft, diffused light to reach
the model from an angle of about forty-five de-
grees top and side, giving a good exposure and
developing thoroughly.   By this means he brings
out every shade of detail possible, so that when he
commences to retouch the negative he has some-
thing to work upon, and is able to modify the nose
to any extent.   The lady is naturally gratified, because her photographer has taken the most pleasing view of her face.   It is not always important,
nor yet advisable, to flatter a lady's portrait; but
no harm is ever done by choosing the more favorable view and better side of the face, bringing forth
those points which are manifestly the most advan-
tageous to the sitter.

Now, as Mr. Brown has given satisfaction, it is
not our purpose to deal with his negative, but
the rejected one of the unfortunate Smith, with a
view to bringing it as near to the same point of
perfection as that of Brown.   The unnatural, badly formed nose he has produced must be convert-
ed or modified to one of the type most suited to

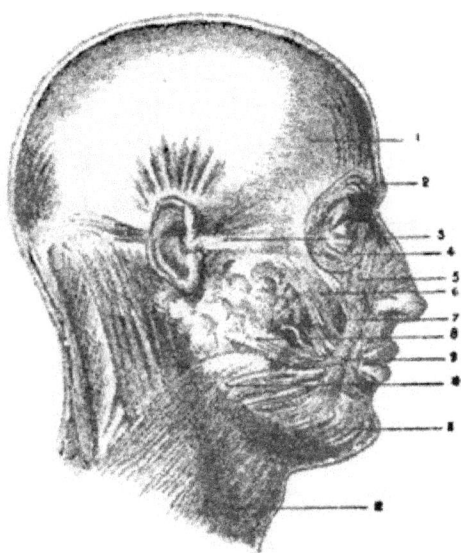

PLATE I

the sitter's peculiar style of beauty—not to alter it into a Roman or an aquiline nose, which would be as great a mistake as that already made, but to modify it by approaching slightly to whichever of these would, without any alteration of the likeness, produce a more pleasing picture, always being careful to leave no possibility of the departure from nature being perceived. As this lady's nose is *retroussé*, the rest of her features will be, no doubt, in keeping, seeing which the retoucher is to make it correspond or harmonize with the rest of the face.

This is not at all times an easy matter, but can be accomplished in most cases by a little judicious working, as we shall describe when speaking of this part of the face.

A practice prevalent among photographers of under-development of negatives is much to be deprecated, as tending to increase the labor of the retoucher. Many photographers seem afraid of their developer, allowing it to remain upon the plate so little time that all the imperfections, such

as deep lines, freckles, etc., which with proper development appear semi-transparent, are absolutely
clear glass ; others, under the impression that they
are using a lightning process, under-expose, and
finish the damage thus commenced by using too
strong a developer, in the hope of bringing out
details they are conscious of having exposed too
briefly to impress upon the film. The development should be carried on until the details are
well out, and the freckles, etc., partially subdued.
In badly freckled faces, the development may be
carried much farther than usual.

An excellent way of subduing freckles is to
wash the face in warm water just before sitting,
or to rub well with a rough towel. This makes
the surrounding portions of the face red, and as
the freckles are yellow, by giving a little longer
exposure than usual, they will be scarcely visible
in the negative. Even in the worst cases they
are so much reduced, and the retoucher's work
consequently so much lessened, that the photographer is fully compensated for his extra trouble.

The face may also be well powdered, which will greatly reduce the exposure.

When retouching freckles and deep lines, it is often found a difficult matter to get the pencil to take, in parts that have been once touched, the pencil having so glazed the surface upon its first application that further density with lead cannot be given. For this reason it is necessary for the operator to be able to judge pretty nearly of the work needed, in order that he may get as much lead on with the first stroke as the spot will require. When a retouching medium is used upon the unvarnished film, after as much as can be put on the film is finished, the negative may be varnished, the surface then abraded or treated with the resin solution and the face reworked upon the varnish.

Rembrandt negatives must be treated rather differently to those ordinarily lighted, for in these more than in others, the distorting effect of improper lighting is very apparent. The nose is by no means the only part of the face which be-

comes distorted or exaggerated, and which requires very careful manipulation and much experience to restore to its true form. All freckles,
lines, comedones or black heads and marks of
every description are exaggerated in this style of
lighting to a far greater extent than in ordinarily
lighted negatives. These defects are again frequently made more glaring by under-exposure
and over-intensification, producing too strong contrasts. A tendency to hardness should always be
overcome by the retoucher when it is not possible
for him to govern the photographer, though the
latter is the one to obviate this defect ; and as it
can at no time be overcome so well as during the
operations of exposure and development, it should
then receive attention.

In elderly persons, the lines of the face and
texture of the skin are much deepened, particularly when a top light has been used.

A distressing negative for a hardly worked retoucher, is one which has been focussed pretty well
to the front, and a small diaphragm used in the

lens. Such a one will be found to be extremely troublesome, requiring the most skillful working to make a presentable picture.

The labial furrow (No. 5, Pl. 2)—the line running from the nose to the corner of the mouth—is always deeper on the light than on the shadow side of face, from the fact that in the one on the shadow side, running in the same direction as the light in which the picture is taken, the light enters it and brightens it up ; whereas, on the other or light side the light crosses the direction of the furrow, which, being shielded by the muscle over it, *Nasilis Labii Superioris*, the common elevator of the *Ala* (No. 7, Pl. 1) no light enters. The same rule applies in a measure to all other lines, though not to such a marked degree ; hence the shadow side of a face always contains less modelling and half tone, but, being in shadow, it can be improved or rectified by skillful working. Upon this point most beginners fail at first to satisfy themselves with their work, and yet a moment's reflection should show them at once where the fault lies,

which, in most instances, consists in their filling up
the entire shadow side, half tone and all, making it
as smooth as they know how, and then adding a
high light to correspond, as they think, with the
other side of the face.   They forget to consider
that the light does not strike both sides alike
Due regard must also be given to perspective ;
muscles, etc., seen from one point differ materially
from those seen from another point of view, both
in appearance and lighting.   When reflectors are
used (which, if employed, should be so placed as
to avoid strong reflection and false lights) there is
often a false light produced in the eyes, more particularly that upon the shadow side or next the
reflector.   This is impossible to remove nicely in
the negative, and it must be touched out upon the
print.   Methods are given by some retouchers to
do this, but as they are neither clean nor certain,
it is best to leave it to the spotter to remove.

Properly speaking, false lights of any kind should
not exist.   Another thing the retoucher has to accustom himself to, is to be able to tell, upon seeing

any unusually deep lines or peculiar marks, whether they are photographic exaggerations or really
characteristic points of the subject, and, if exaggerations, to decide what extent of modification they
will bear without destroying the character of the
face upon which he is at work. A mole or scar,
for instance, will usually be exaggerated, but if
fully removed, the likeness would suffer a little
loss; and as a number of little departures from
truth would soon totally obliterate all likeness, it
is better to indulge in none.

The license of successful artistic portraiture
permits a representation as favorable to the sitter
as possible; there is, nevertheless, a limit to flat-
tery which is only definable by peculiar circumstances of the case, as with personal imperfections
a resemblance can often be secured without signalizing the blemish, and even when this is impossible, it is by no means illegitimate practice to
subdue it, if done with discretion, taking care to
preserve distinctive impersonation.

The hair, hands, and drapery should also receive an adequate share of attention, though these portions of a negative do not require such elaborate work as the face ; at the same time what is done must be done carefully, and with the same light and shade effect as the rest of the picture.

The hands, unless nicely formed, in good focus and well posed, should always be as subdued as possible, and in no instance should either the hand or any accessory be more prominent, or attract the eye more, than the face.   This should be the main feature of all negatives, the remaining portions being simply arranged and kept partly subdued. When the face is not the most attractive part in the negative, the retoucher must always intensify it by means of plumbago applied at the back ; and when portions are too bright, they may be greatly reduced by rendering the matt varnish transparent with turpentine varnish or dammar varnish. A diversity of effect may be obtained by lightening parts of the background, a surprising difference being easily obtainable with a few tasteful touches on the back, with a stump charged with plumbago, soft pastel powder, or crayon sauce.

With landscape negatives, the retoucher has generally but little to do ; but it is well to know what to do when one has them. As, however, little work is required, if worth doing at all it is worth doing well. More credit is due to a man who can make a passable picture of an indifferent negative, than to one who produces good work having always a negative of the best quality and most suitable to retouch. This is not intended to imply that landscape negatives are usually indifferent ; but it seldom happens that the retoucher has anything to do with really good ones, whereas upon the less perfect ones the lights have often to be put in or existing lights subdued, the cloud effects to be made to harmonize with the rest of the picture, and, in most cases, the whole of the sky to be worked in.

This is frequently done by combination printing (of which mention is made in another chapter) ; but this plan is often impracticable, and the sky is

left to the resources of the retoucher to do the
best that is possible with it.   Mentioning this may
seem superfluous; but these things must all be
known to the pupil before attempting to retouch.
as it is of little use working upon what one does
not thoroughly understand, or trying to make im-
provements without a knowledge of what they are
to be.

CHAPTER II.

The Materials and Their Selection.

THE requirements of the retoucher, are a retouching desk, a supply of pencils of various grades, a magnifying glass, several small brushes, stumps of paper and leather, a few cakes of water color, viz., neutral tint, Indian red and carmine, and a bottle of a good, hard matt varnish, one which dries quickly with an even matt surface, and upon which work can be done with the harder grades of pencils.

The negative should be fully exposed, thin and full of detail ; over-dense negatives are at all times unsatisfactory to work upon. Unfortunately it is not always the retoucher's fortune to get negatives possessing such degree of excellence as he would wish, in fact, it is the practice of many operators to allow indifferent ones to pass, consoling themselves with the thought that the retoucher can make all defects good. This is to be regretted, being by no means conducive to the production of good work or advancement of the art ; it is, however, the case, and being so, we must resort to the readiest means of correcting the error. This view is taken from the standpoint of a professional retoucher, who receives daily many negatives from different operators and employs a number of skilled assistants, a steady increase of business being sufficient guarantee of his ability to speak authoritatively.

If it be intended to work the negative upon the varnish, it will be necessary to abrade its surface with cuttle-fish powder, or some other abrading substance, to cause the pencil to bite. This slight matter, which would appear so simple, is by no means the least important, and requires to be done systematically and with the same amount of attention as any of the subsequent operations. Care being taken that no gritty particles are in the powder employed (which would scratch the film). Place as much on the face as will cover a dime and proceed gently to grind the surface with the ball of the finger—not in a circular motion, as would be the most usual course, but more up and down the face, the course of the finger describing ellipses, the greater diameters of which are down the face. The surface thus produced, takes the lead better and gives a finer touch than circular abrasion. Rub very carefully, holding the negative in such a position as to be able to see that the powder is not cutting through the film, and until it feels tolerably rough; a little practice will be necessary to enable one to distinguish when the right condition is obtained. Examine with a magnifying glass from time to time to see that the peculiar tooth which indicates the proper surface is produced, perfectly matt and containing no shiny patches; now dust off the superfluous powder with a soft brush and wipe from the parts not to be retouched. If not sufficiently abraded, repeat the operation, as this precaution may often save the retoucher from removing all his work in consequence of the pencil refusing to take in some parts, necessitating the entire re-abrasion of the negative.

Various gums and solutions are employed in place of powder to give a tooth to the film ; these may answer for some kinds of varnish, but as an abrading material, cuttle-fish will be found more generally useful.   The most useful solution where abrading is not advisable (as for negatives intended for subsequent enlarging, etc.) is a simple solution of common resin in turpentine; the author has used this for the past two years upon every variety of varnish to be had in the American market. and finds no cause to complain of its general utility.   Solar prints or enlargements made from negatives retouched upon it, show none of the markings usually met with when a small negative has been abraded.   Negatives that have been retouched upon an abraded surface and required for enlargement, may be improved by having some of this solution rubbed over the abraded portions ; this will prevent the lines from showing.

A saturated solution of the resin in turpentine should be kept on hand, and the clear portion diluted by twice its bulk for use. Formulæ for other solutions will be found in another chapter, each of which the retoucher may try, selecting one which answers his touch best. It seldom happens that two retouchers can at first use precisely the same materials for working, as they may not have the same touch. The more delicately the work upon a negative is to be done, the finer and at the same time the more abraded or matt must be the surface. This is why retouching upon unvarnished films is so much finer and softer than that done upon varnish, the matt surface of the collodion, which has been hardened or tanned by any reliable means, being so exquisitely fine that it may be worked upon to any extent, having a tooth which takes the pencil as readily as paper. As touching upon such films requires very delicate

work (on account of the facility with which lead
may be put on, a novice is apt to do too much),
the beginner is advised to commence his studies
upon varnish, until he accustoms himself to handle
the pencil in such a way as to produce a light,
feathery stroke; for, although working on the film
is decidedly more pleasant and expeditious, and
negatives so treated produce superior prints, it
takes much longer to learn upon films than upon
varnish. Having once mastered the art upon varnish, very little practice is required to attain proficiency in working upon the medium.

Another reason why the beginner should use
varnish until he can make sure of his touch is, that
not being thoroughly accustomed to the work he
is constantly making mistakes, or finds when his
negative is printed that he has done too much
upon it which will have to be removed. Upon
varnish, this can be done by re-abrasion of the surface, but upon the film, a stroke once made is permanently fixed and cannot be removed. In such
cases the employment of the turpentine solution is

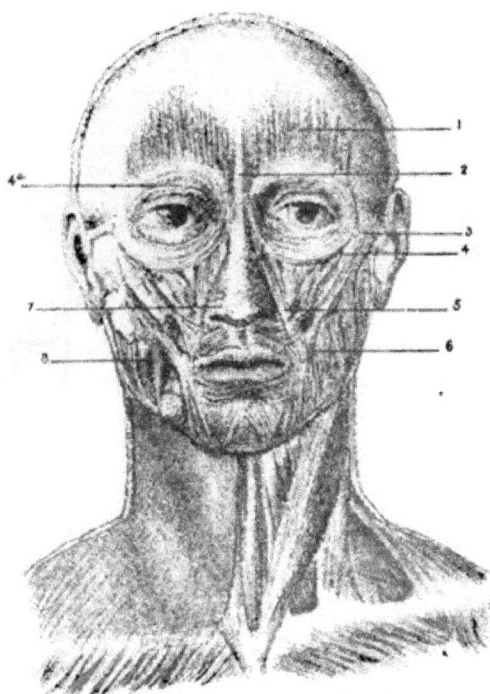

PLATE 2.

advisable, as it affords greater facility of touching over and over upon one head until perfection is attained, by simply removing the work with a wad of cotton charged with turpentine and applying more medium as directed, proceeding as before, carefully noting previous errors and avoiding a repetition of them.

PENCILS.

In selecting pencils, the greatest pains should be taken and the greatest difficulty will be found, as few makers produce leads of an uniform quality. Those used for retouching must be of the finest and closest manufacture possible to procure, well moulded, and absolutely free from grit. For general work, Siberian leads HHH or HHHH will be found the most suitable grades, using a harder one for fine dotting and upon those parts which require but a light touch.

Having procured your pencils, proceed to sharpen them by cutting away the wood, leaving about one half an inch of the lead free to be point-

ed.   Rub the lead away upon a piece of glass-
paper until it has a very sharp, long and slender
point.   The wood must be cut away rather ob-
tusely, to prevent it obstructing the sight while
being used, thus :

We now allude, of course, to the ordinary wood-
cased pencils.   In our own practice we much prefer using those known as "Eagle Automatic
Holders."   These are to be had at any station-
er's, the advantages in their use being that they
are always the same length and are less ex-
pensive than the other forms.   One holder is sufficient for all purposes, the leads being changed as
they are needed.   Leads of various grades should
always be kept in readiness for use, as the character of negative or circumstances may require.
We shall describe the different methods employed
and which have come under our notice, pointing
out, at the same time, their respective merits or

disadvantages. We must again remind the reader in passing, to adhere strictly to one method,
whichever he proposes to learn, until perfect in
it, before attempting a second style, otherwise the
object aimed at in this book will be lost.

The Light.

The light by which negatives are to be worked must necessarily be a good one   By this we
do not mean to be understood a very powerful,
glaring light, although it should be sufficiently
strong to show all the defects in the negative
when reflected through it by means of a suitable
reflector.   The usual plan of retouching desk fitted only with a plain mirror, which has to be
used near a window, has the disadvantage of a
false, glaring light which in time impairs the sight,
and, at the same time, does not give as satisfactory
results as could be wished for.   This defect may
be obviated to a great extent by suspending a
ground glass at half the angle formed by the mir-

ror and middle frame of the desk when opened,
thus :

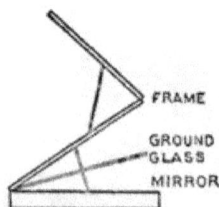

A piece of ordinary glass coated with matt varnish will answer the purpose as well as, if not better than, ground glass ; besides, it is not as expen-
sive, and if broken can be replaced at a very trifling cost.

THE MAGNIFIER.

The magnifying-glass used, should be of about
six inches focal length and preferably, from three
and a half to four inches in diameter, to enable
the operator to see through it with both eyes. It
should be fixed in some such way that it may be
always used at the same distance from the negative
and in the same position ; for, if held in the hand,
it is liable to such constant vibration—causing

the eye to incessantly change focus to accommo-
date itself to the moving glass—that in a short
time the sight may become permanently impair-
ed. This is particularly the case with persons
whose eyes have a tendency to dilation of the
cornea.

THE DESK.

There are many forms of desks in use for negative retouching. Those generally employed are
fitted with carriers or frames to take the different
sizes of photographic plates. The desk itself consists of three frames hinged together, with a plate
of silvered glass embedded in the lower frame to
reflect the light. The carriers are rebated to fit
in the middle frame, and the upper frame is made
solid, to prevent the light reaching the retoucher's
eyes. The upper and middle frames are support-
ed in position by means of light iron bars, which
fit into notches at the lower ends; the bar itself
lies in a groove when the desk is closed.

The annexed sketch will give an idea of the
sort of apparatus of which we speak.

Another form is also used answering the same purpose, in which the carriers are replaced by a

plain sheet of glass, which permits of the different sizes of negatives being worked without the removal of carriers or frames.

Some of the desks of this description have a horizontal bar, at the ends of which are two pegs with nuts and thumb-screws. These pegs slide in grooves or slots in the side of the frame, being held in position by tightening the thumb-screws. The negative is placed upon the sheet of glass, the lower edge resting upon the cross-bar, by means of which it is kept in any desired position. The desk should have an attachment for holding the magnifier in a fixed position at a suitable distance from the negative, and in such a position as not to interfere with the right arm. The eye is thus spared the exertion of accommodating itself to the ever-changing focus resulting from the magnifier being held in the hand, which injures the sight very much, as indeed must be patent to anyone who gives the subject slight consideration. Of course to the amateur, this is not a matter of much interest, nor even to professionals who only retouch a few negatives daily ; but, to the retoucher who is seated at the retouching desk from morning until night and duly impressed with the fact that no one possessed of the best eyesight can hope to retain it unimpaired after a few years of constant employment at this occupation, it becomes one of vital importance.

This is not advanced simply as a passing remark, but as an absolute fact based upon long practice ; and our opinion on this head will be shared by all whose experience places them in a position to judge.   Professionals and indeed amateurs are recommended to work with as little light as possible, and to allow the light to pass only through that portion of the negative which is being retouched.   The desk should be fitted with an appliance which will enable the retoucher to regulate the amount of light passing through the negative, as circumstances and the strength of the negative may require. A sliding screen fitted at the back of the desk containing squares of glass of different grades, plain, finely ground and opal or porcelain will be found excellent. By sliding this screen to bring different glasses opposite the negative, always examining after retouching through the next deeper degree of opacity, the effect is seen in a moment.

A negative retouched over ground glass, will give through opal, just the appearance the finished print will have ; thus, in stopping out a scar or other defect, one is able to judge more correctly how the work will print, than if it were examined only through plain glass.

For working at night, a violet glass should be used together with the porcelain.

CHAPTER III.

The Face, Hands, Drapery, etc.

THE FACE GENERALLY.

THIS being the principal part of the negative to which attention is to be given, and upon which the whole beauty of a picture depends, we shall treat upon it at length, trusting that our readers may not become weary of the description and pass over our observations hurriedly, as we shall not mention any points which are not really important and which the beginner should not carefully study.

As we have before remarked, and as the pupil will readily understand, each face requires special treatment, from the fact that in all nature, no two

faces are alike. It is not meant by this that each
and every face will require special study, but each
peculiar type or class. In treating of the muscles
and lines of the face to be retouched, we find the
most convenient and comprehensive plan to be
that of referring to a lettered plate, and to be, in
fact, the only way of clearly explaining our mean-
ing without employing unnecessary tautology.
An inspection of our plate will show the principal
muscles and lines to be found in every face, although some of them may not be quite so con-
spicuous in one person as another, from the fact
that they are subdued in a great measure by the
predominance of surrounding parts. This is particularly noticeable in elderly persons, and more
in men than in women. It would seem a fallacy
to assert that in the face of an elderly person the
muscles are not so apparent as in younger ones.
It would be said, perhaps, that the older a person
grows the more prominently his features, etc., are
marked. This may be true as concerns the folds
and wrinkles, but the muscles themselves are not

so clearly defined ; and for this reason it is not only the muscles which are to be studied, but their contractions and movements, as these latter form most of the lines to be treated.

As an example of this we will take the buccinator of the intermaxillary group ; that is to say, the space between the jaws and the circumference of the mouth, and that corresponding with the lower jaw (*Zygomato-maxillaris*). In a young person these muscles are very pronounced ; but in elderly ones the subcutaneous fat immediately under the skin disappears in proportion to the age of the person, and the integumentary covering, having lost its contractibility, does not return to its usual form as in youth, but remains in folds, and falls to such an extent as to entirely alter the shape as well as the expression of this part of the face. The same may be said of the *palpebral* region (No. 4 and 4A, Pl. 2) ; that is, the circumference of the eye, eyebrows, etc., which changes its form to a greater extent, perhaps, than the others. The labial furrow (No. 5, Pl. 2) becomes

very decided when the flesh loses consistency in
the manner above mentioned. These lines must
not be totally obliterated nor too much softened.
Certainly a person is made to look much younger
by such treatment, as, of course, it subdues the
loose flesh, thereby showing more distinctly the
formation of the muscles ; still it destroys the true
character of the face. The folds and wrinkles in
the skin, which are caused by contraction of the
muscles, run always in a perpendicular direction to
the muscles themselves and cross their direction,
such as those in the forehead. The frontal depression in a child is scarcely marked ; but as he
or she grows older, and the muscles, *Orbisculares
Palpebrarum* (No. 4A, Pl. 2), are constantly contracted, a furrow forms across the forehead between these muscles above the nose, continuing
up to between the frontals (fig. 1, Pl. 2).

With respect to men whose foreheads are
marked at an early age by much study, physical
and moral sufferings, etc., the wrinkle, if not sufficiently retouched in the negative, would give a

much older appearance to the portrait than that in actual life, from the cause we have already explained ; that is, the light crossing the direction of the wrinkle would make it appear more deeply set than was natural.

The frontal depression (fig. 2, Pl. 2), or the furrow in the forehead at the root of the nose, may be so treated as to give or disperse an expression of grief, pain, or frowning. It is sometimes only a single and very slight furrow ; but in men much employed in intellectual labors, there are generally two folds decidedly marked, and at the sides of these folds are two small protuberances, which should in no case be obliterated, while at times it is even advisable to increase their size somewhat by introducing a little light upon them. This modification may be resorted to with advantage in the case of negatives of persons whose eyes are farther apart than the average, and whose foreheads are low and flat or receding.

To begin with the forehead and work down the face, in the same manner as it is retouched, will be the simplest way to proceed with our description.

The frontal eminences, which we always make the starting-point, are two prominences on the upper part of the forehead above the orbits and superciliary arches. They appear usually as two, but occasionally the depression separating them is so slight as to make the two appear as one large protuberance. In extreme youth they are always more pronounced; that is to say, the projection is greater, but, owing to the fresh, pulpy condition of the covering, the depression dividing them is not so decided. They must be smoothed and softened by very careful retouching, and brightened so as to appear the most pronounced high lights of the face (with the exception of the sharp line of light upon the nose), due care being taken to light them in proper perspective, and to give to the one nearer the source of light the greater prominence. A great fault often lies in placing the high light too near the centre of the forehead and too high up and near the hair.

It must always be borne in mind that rotundity
is best obtained by placing the densest lights in
the centre of the high lights, and the deepest portions of shadows in the centre of shades, never
allowing the edge of a light or shadow to be
sharp or defined.   Immediately under, over, and
between these lights a delicate half tone must be
left. The lower one must gradually increase in
intensity as it approaches the orbitar arches or
brows, where it is again worked into high light.
From the outer edge of the frontals the forehead
recedes, forming the half flat temporal surface,
which must always be left a half tone slightly
deeper than that between the frontals and orbits.
This throws the frontals and orbits up and gives
life and form to the eyes.   There exists in muscular and thin persons a curved line or crest,
which must be to an extent subdued.   The malar
or cheek bone (No. 6, Pl. 1) must be lightened
and led into the cheek, the highest point of its
light being under the eye, immediately over the
highest point of the malar bone. As the bone

approaches the ear it should be only slightly worked and made less pronounced; the concha or funnel-shaped entrance to the ear may receive a very slight light upon the upper edge of the cartilaginous protuberance, remembering what has been said about placing lights too near the edge.

Having made this part sufficiently even, we now return to the frontal depression at the root of the nose, which must be kept subdued, simply evening it and removing too strong furrows running across the top of the nose The upper lids of the eyes should be very cautiously touched, taking care to destroy none of the lines formed by the elevation of the lid.

The Eye is the dominant feature, and its expression precedes even the language of the lips in challenging the attention of the spectator. This organ is too often overlooked by retouchers and photographers, probably more because of the difficulty of treating it properly. We desire at this point, as we are aiming at making first-class retouchers of our readers, to direct special attention

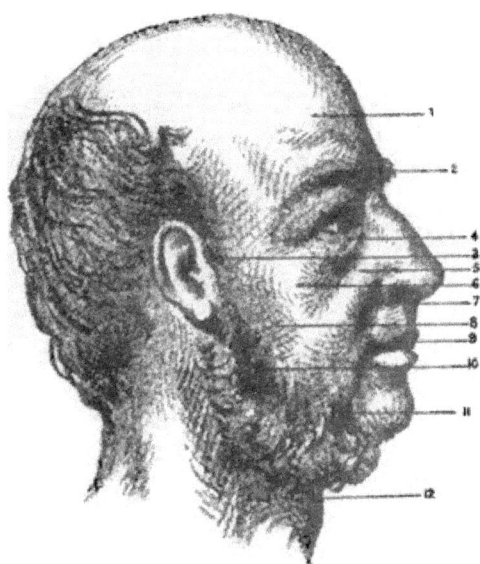

PLATE 3.

to the differences in shape assumed by the eye at various periods of life; a knowledge of where to look for these changes must be acquired, for it is better to leave the eye untouched than to attempt it without such knowledge.

The progress from childhood to youth is indicated in the inner angle of the eye, while as life advances these changes are to be found at the outer corner. The difference of character between the eye of a man and that of a woman should not be overlooked; the eye of the latter must be represented in all softness and brilliancy, only for the expression of tender sentiment, while all that is epic and philosophical is becoming in the eye of a man.

The eye of a lady should generally be treated as in full light, to demonstrate all its characteristic delicacy of construction; when photographed in such light as to show the detail of structure, the desire to intensify all the perceptible niceties of form will often lead the student astray, for even were he to succeed in detailing all the little feath-

ery forms noticeable, it would be impossible to
handle them with sufficient accuracy of relative
density to preserve the expression, and would be
useless in small portraits; on the other hand it is
impossible to treat large light and shade portraits
by simple allusion—where the rendition of minute detail is not necessary to resemblance, it may
be simply indicated—but light and shade demand
the most scrupulous truth and justice in their
treatment.   In negatives where every minute
portion of the structure of the eye is visible, every
line must be rendered, but without any degree of
spottiness or severity signalizing certain points,
which cannot be subdued without injury to resemblance.   Such treatment results in breadth
and effect when successfully carried out.   A light
so high as to throw the eye into strong shade, is
not a favorable one in which to photograph aged
persons, as it signalizes too strongly the indications of age, not alone in the eye but wherever
its traces most prominently exist.   When such a
light is used, however, breadth must be preserved

by guarding against dark spots upon broad lights
and subduing bright spots in the middle of dark
tints and half tones.

Every part of the eye must be accurately adjusted to convey impressions of vitality and in-
telligence. The light reflected in the eye must
be many tones higher than that of any other part,
still preserving harmony with surrounding portions. The eyebrow in dark complexions must
not be retouched to form a hard and solid mass ;
retouching the flesh in a sharp line up to the
brow will produce this defect.

Our cautionary remarks against severity of line
in drawing, applies equally to every other part of
the face in many portraits, exceptions to the rule
being subjects after the middle age, principally in
men ; where these peculiar characteristics exist
they must be brought forward with caution. The
brow may be bushy, or here and there tufted, or
the hair fail ; these points must be represented by
spirited touches with a soft blunt pencil, as any attempt to individualize the hairs will result in failure.

The upper lash is a striking feature upon which much of the character of the eye depends, while the lower lash does not in any way contribute to the marking of the eye.

Two common errors with beginners must be particularly guarded against, that of marking the eyelash too strongly and that of obliterating them completely, making the eye look as if it had been singed.   The upper edge of the lash must be softened into the lid, and the lower edge must melt imperceptibly into the shadows which it casts upon the orb beneath it.   Under the outward extremity of the lash, the thickness of the lid is perceptible; this must be represented as it is seen, that is, distinct from the lash and tender in tone. The form assumed by the pupil of the eye is of course governed by the relative position of the head—round in full face portraits and oval in profile, intermediate forms with half profile, three-quarter face, etc.   These positions in turn, control the lighting of the eye.

The following remarks will treat different points

of the eye more locally and will guide the beginner by progressive steps until complete. Commence to retouch the organ by placing a light
upon the top light side of the iris. This light will
be but a wedge-shaped speck, and directly opposite to it in the direction of the source of light
there must be a longer light much lower in tone,
about the third of a circle in form, taking the
same curved direction as the iris; this will render
the luminous effect produced by the light passing
through the convex form of the eye. Place a
light in the lower light side of the white fibrous
membrane—the *Sclerotic*—cautiously avoiding
blocking up the shadow formed by the upper
eyelid. A small white speck placed in the extreme corner on the shadow side at the intersec-
tion of the lids—the *Caruncular Lachrymalis*—
and a few judicious touches on the edges of the
lids where the lashes begin, leaving the dark
spaces formed by the lashes untouched, finish the
eye and greatly improve the life and expression
of the negative.

Let us here exhort the student to avoid falling
into an error not only made by beginners but
persisted in by many retouchers of long experience, that is, of destroying the extremely delicate
transparency of the skin immediately under the
eye; every little prevailing tint should be carefully preserved, and will materially help to give
expression to the eye. The lower lid has generally two or three sharp lines under or upon it, and
a furrow under it, which is very much increased
by sorrow, age, pain, or excessive pleasure.

This furrow must be very much subdued, not
totally removed, as an indication of it must always
remain to help the eye; those above it, however,
will require very little modification, and if too
much diminished they give a dead appearance to
the eye. We have now finished with confessedly
the most difficult organ. We trust our remarks
are comprehensive, as we have intended them to
be; and with the assurance that we have consci-
entiously described the full manipulation of the
eye, as the author himself has been accustomed to

treat it, we will pass to another organ, which is
altogether neglected by retouchers generally and
not only by them but by most photographers—
in our opinion it is deserving of just as much attention as any other part of the head.

The Ear, as we have just said, is frequently
treated with indifference not only by retouchers
and photographers but by many artists.   An inspection of the productions of eminent workers
will, however, convince one that the ear has been
made the subject of most accurate study.   It may
be said in palliation of the neglect of this organ
that, being without expression and not an intellectual feature, it does not contribute to resemblance.   The former we are quite willing to ad-
mit, but in the latter opinion we can by no means
concur.

That all ears are not alike is sufficient to in-
sure them some attention ; and this fact is also
proof that the ears do frequently contribute to
resemblance   When, therefore, this feature is
represented in full light, as in three-quarter face

and profile portraits, it should be treated with the utmost precision, and by judicious disposition the exaggerations of photography usually apparent in the ear should be modified. The softness of the lobe should be fully described and the upper cartilaginous surfaces tenderly treated.

In three-quarter and front views, the retouching of the ear may be made to contribute much to the perspective, while in profile portraits it may be so handled as to give breadth. It is not an unusual thing to see the ear of a grown person so distorted as to appear quite round, like that of a child. As the ear elongates with age, this defect should be modified by increasing all perpendicular cartilaginous lights to give less breadth and better form to the ear.

At the side of the nose above the labial furrow will be found the common elevator muscle of the *Ala* of the nose and upper lip. This may be lightened to a certain extent in the middle, but care must be taken not to carry the light too close to the nose, as the nearer it is to that feature

the flatter and broader the nose appears. While
working upon this muscle the labial furrow must
be softened to the extent required, taking it nearly all away as it joins the nose and gradually running into it.

Many Americans are peculiar in having no
labial furrow. Such subjects are difficult to treat
properly. The absence of this furrow makes the
nose appear much larger, and this defect is exaggerated by photography. Malays, Indians, and
Swedes also possess this peculiarity in majority.

Should the sitter have assumed a pouting, dis-
agreeable expression, by which the furrow is
made to curve down towards the mouth, its direction may be somewhat changed by removing
the lower curved end of the line and leaving
a portion of the face comparatively untouched,
where the end of the line should have been to
have given a pleasing expression. By placing a
little light over this untouched part and rounding
the muscle somewhat, the line will print as if
curved up, which, to say the least, will improve the

expression of the mouth. When this change is resorted to, the crow-foot lines or furrows at the corners of the eyes may be allowed partly to remain, as also the round shadow at the corner of the mouth, all of which aid in rendering the desired expression. The shadow at the corner of the mouth can be increased by contrast by making a semi-circular light around it.

The retoucher must aim to be consistent in working, and, when an alteration to an agreeable expression is attempted in the mouth, the eyes and cheeks must coincide in the same feeling.

On the upper lip, in the centre, is a groove which terminates in the septum of the nose; the projecting edges of this groove must be brightened, the light increasing as it approaches the end at the edge of the lip. The light upon the light side of this groove must be a little longer than the one on the shadow side, as the nose throws a shade over the latter which must not be disturbed at this point.

The Mouth. It must not be forgotten when

treating the mouth that its form is no less susceptible to the changes of time, etc., at different periods of life than other features. In infancy its round and contracted form and beauty of construction must not be tampered with by too great freedom in the employment of high lights.

The mouths of infants assist only in a very small degree in expression. Young children smile and laugh almost exclusively with their eyes. But as teeth make their appearance, the mouth finds other offices to fill besides the extraction of nourishment, and its form changes, becoming more and more elongated with the growth of the teeth, and coincides more in expression with the eyes. Age produces another and equally remarkable change, and as the teeth begin to disappear, the mouth loses its power of varying expression. These things must all be borne in mind when attempting to beautify or flatter a negative. If the retoucher familiarizes himself with these changes he will find no difficulty in imparting a youthful appearance to a negative, when required, without making the alteration apparent ; that is to say, it will please the sitter because it looks a little more youthful, and yet if it were attempted to point out the difference between the picture and sitter it would be found impossible by taking each feature individually.

A light should also be placed near the upper edge at the centre of the lower lip, just sufficient to give form and expression to the mouth. It must have two intense portions in its length to carry out the double bow form. We speak of two intense portions merely by contrast to the rest of the light, as actually the entire light must be faint though graded. A light should also be placed upon the upper edge, near the centre of the lower lip ; this light must be very faint, just sufficient to give form and expression to the mouth.

The lips themselves will sometimes be found to have small downward depressions caused by the skin having become dry or cracked. Should this be noticed at the time of sitting a request should be made to the sitter to moisten the lips in the usual manner; but if from any cause they remain, and are visible in the negative, they must be wholly removed.

The shadow under the lower lip will require but little work, being simply softened and led into the chin to avoid too much rotundity or projection.

The Chin may be said to be a difficult feature to handle with judgment. Chins vary so much in form that each one requires separate study. It should generally be brought forward with its due importance, but an incidental characteristic which points to an unfavorable allusion should be subdued; a very flat or a greatly elongated chin should not be too predominant. The same suggestion applies to wrinkles in the brow or even dimples in the cheek of youth; it is a mistake to assert that because they are strongly marked in nature they should be so represented in portraits, for however skilled the operator may be, and however much he may have succeeded in overcoming the anomalies of photography, he still cannot make his portrait a living creature, and, until he can, all blemishes will appear more pronounced than in nature.

The chin, although varying in form, is generally nearly round, with a slight indentation in the centre. The light must never be very strong upon this feature, and when the chin is square its form will have to be suggested in the lighting. Having finished so much of the face, give the lower jaw a little light, evening up all inequalities and harmonizing it with the work already done, and all that remains is to place the lights upon the nose and to remove markings in the neck.

The Nose. The light upon the nose will have to be very carefully worked or else the rest of the work, however nicely done, will be greatly deteriorated. We have seen many negatives otherwise fairly retouched, hopelessly spoiled, as far as the likeness was concerned, by the introduction of a line of light entirely out of character with the feature itself, and, in fact, completely altering its shape.

Some retouchers seem to labor under the impression that a patch of light on the forehead, and a straight line terminating in a spot or bulb of light at the end of the nose, are essentials in every case.

If the end or lobe be of double form—which, however, is never very apparent—the light will have to be sharper, or, rather, more angular ; the longer the light along its side the longer the nose will appear. By making this high light more intense and broader at the middle, the nose will be a better shape. Upon the wings or sesamoid cartilage (No. 1, Pl. 2) a round, very soft, and diffused light, just a shade removed from half tone, should be placed, and when indicated in the negative, the inner surface of the nostril may receive a light touch to relieve the intense shadow. When the nose has been distorted by improper lighting, as mentioned in a previous chapter, let the rest of the face be worked with rather more density than usual, and increase its opacity with plumbago at the back. The nose will now appear comparatively dark, and may be worked upon to any extent. The bulb must receive a sharp angular light, and the bridge be lightened by a short, slightly curved line, about the same density as the light upon the bulb. The edges of this light must be softened, and led into the half tone between it and the cheek.

The Neck seldom requires much retouching, except in portraits of ladies wearing low-necked dresses or bodices. All deep furrows should be removed and a soft light placed upon the muscles and clavicle—the clavicle in ladies of spare habit is apt to be too conspicuously defined ; this must all be very cautiously subdued. The general tone of neck and shoulders should be of a lower key than that of the face, the highest light of which is the forehead. In men, the larynx generally throws too deep a shadow, which should be softened, and the muscles are too obviously demonstrated ; the light, however, must not be touched, as it would throw the throat too much forward.

The hair may be improved by working upon

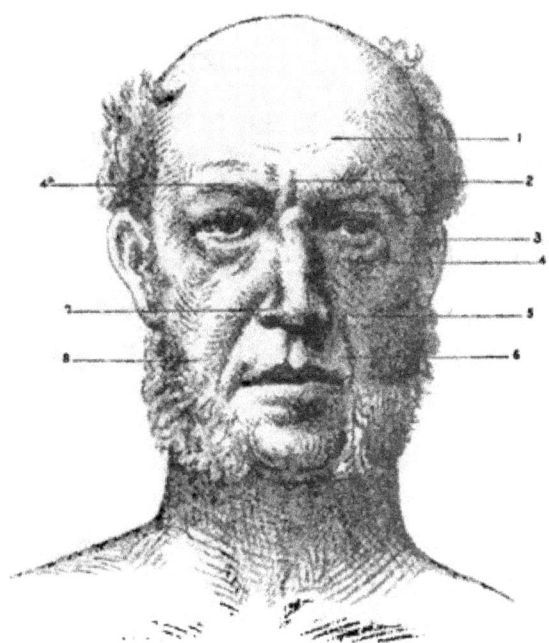

PLATE 4

the lights and blending them with the shadows, using for the purpose a blunt and soft pencil. At the edges, the hair should be led into and given the value of the retouching done upon the face ; this is to avoid too abrupt contour lines, bearing in mind that roundness is always secured by soft contours and brilliant centres, and not by violent contrasts. The hair may be lightened all over by applying ivory black or plumbago at the back of the negative upon matt varnish. If the hair take too darkly, a better effect may be produced by powdering it at the time of sitting. The broad lights in the face, as we have mentioned before, are also put in, in this manner.

The hands and arms in ladies' portraits, when shown, will require to be worked up to subdue the heavy veins, which usually appear more prominently than in nature. The creases on the knuckles should be removed and the luna in nails strengthened. Unless the hands are very small and very well posed they should be always as much subdued as possible.

In painting, the hand is one of the most difficult exercises of the artist's skill, and we see no
reason why a little more care should not be be-
stowed upon it than is usually seen in photography. Few retouchers study the hand at all,
and those who do, generally dispose of it in a
slovenly, sketchy style by which it is not much
improved; but we have never failed to find that
the most elaborate accuracy in treatment always
repaid us. Whether such careful work would pay
commercially is not for us to say; we only pro-
pose showing what should be done to produce
the best work.

It is a significant fact that the best photographers, who have made world-wide reputations, always pay as much attention to these points as to
the rest of a picture.

Hands and arms should only be seen when
looked for—that is, they must be subdued—but
when looked for they should be found to have received their share of care.

When skillfully disposed they form a powerful

auxiliary in expression of pose ; and if so lighted
in retouching as to give them an easy, probable
and fleshy appearance (not flattened and lightened so as to make them look like either white
marble or cut out white paper), they constitute
an essential part of the study of ladies' portraiture,
with their beauty of proportion and graceful dis-
play of line.

It must not be forgotten that the left hand
bends more gracefully at the wrist than the right,
and the license of art permits a concession to the
right hand of the superior grace of the left. The
characteristics of the different fingers will speak
for themselves in each negative.

The drapery, except in cases of very glossy and
thin silks—which usually appear too much broken
up to receive further manipulation—should be
brightened up to harmonize with the rest of the
picture. Light materials— blue, drab and white—
are by the slightest manipulation made to look so
brilliant, and to contain so much delicate half-tone
and detail, that it amply repays the retoucher to

bestow the little time required upon them, enhancing, as they do, the beauty of the negative. These lights are always indicated in the negative, though not sufficiently strong to print. It only remains, then, to intensify them by means of sharp, decisive touches applied to the back of the negative with a leather stump and plumbago. It need hardly be said that the pupil's knowledge of drawing will greatly assist him to do this. When the negatives are prepared for retouching upon the film, a number of these sharp high lights can be put in upon the film side of the plate, using for the purpose a fine cork or moulded gray paper stump. When the back is shown, as is sometimes done in full-length pictures, avoid the folds or plaits running across the waist of the dress by removing the heavy shadows. Lace of any description is made to look very effective by a few sharp touches, preferably done upon the back of tne negative, using either a soft pencil or white crayon upon matt varnish.

The above observations apply to whichever

method of retouching is employed, as, of course, in each of them the ultimate result is striven for and the same principles of art involved.

CHAPTER IV.

Methods of Working.

FIRST METHOD.

THE first method described will be the one employed by the author in his own practice, and which has given so much satisfaction and received such hearty recommendation from those for whom he has retouched. This refers to an experience of some years as a professional retoucher, with several pupils and assistants always engaged, and, perhaps, a larger number of negatives received daily than ever fell to the lot of any one retoucher.

By preference we take a negative the film of which has been treated, before drying, with a me-

dium of some kind to prevent the pencil going
through, and to give it the necessary tooth for
working upon. Our tannin medium, which has
been for some time in the market, is extensively
used, and will be found to answer the purpose ad-
mirably without the disadvantages attendant upon
the use of gum and other substitutes. Should,
however, the negative have been varnished, much
the same course or mode of working is adopted,
the surface being abraded as described in a previous chapter.

We commence proceedings by placing the negative in such a position as to be able to make
with a downward stroke of the pencil a line across
the forehead. First fill in all irregular and transparent spots and lines (which we have mentioned
in speaking of the face), giving to these spots and
lines the same value as the surrounding portions
of the forehead, beginning at the point of highest
light. The regular lines—that is to say, the per-
manent ones—must not be totally obliterated, as
we have already shown when describing the

muscles, etc.   The spots and irregularities are not
to be completely filled in, as in other processes,
one or two short lines only being drawn through
them.   The object of this is to produce an effect
of stippling upon the finished picture, which could
not be done if the spots were completely blocked,
unless the negative was afterwards stippled all
over.   This would, of course, entail much time,
and the result has only a labored look, without
any of the pleasing, flesh-like stipple always produced when the touches are made as above directed.   The lines and marks made, must take the
same direction as the lines of the skin and direction of the muscles, unless these lines are caused
by the contraction of the muscles, when their
course is perpendicular to and across the muscles.
These lines are, however, but few, occurring principally upon the muscles of the forehead, and occasionally upon the upper lip.   The crow-foot
lines upon the temples are produced in this way,
but are exceptions to the rule, and must not be
removed in every face.   Fill in in a like manner,

with rather longer and more feathery strokes, the
deep lines in the forehead between the frontals
(No. 1, Pl. 2), and the orbitar arches and muscles
(*Orbiscularis Palpebrarum*—No. 4a, Pl. 2). This
must not be done so as to make the entire forehead of one tint ; an indication of these lines may
be left in the first working, and when the breadths
of light are put in, the presence of these indications of form will give a pleasing, transparent, life-
like character to the work difficult to obtain in
any other way. Now turn the negative gradually round, and, still following the direction taken
by the muscle of the orbit, soften the lines upon
the temporal plane. The negative is now turned
farther round until it is nearly upright, in which
position the frontal depression (No. 2, Pl. 2) is
worked, and also the nose, and the negative again
turned back to such a position that the furrows
under the eyes and the common elevator of the
ala, the nose and the upper lip, may be softened
and modelled. The same rules as to the direction of stroke must always be strictly adhered to.

Reference should here be given to remarks on the face in Chapter II.

The strokes in the labial furrow, No. 5, should be made sufficiently dense at the first application, and should run the whole length of the furrow in one sweep of the pencil. Where the lines running in different directions cross or meet each other, the space is filled in with small dots made with the point of the pencil. In this manner we proceed, turning the negative constantly as the lines take a different direction, until the negative appears even and delicate all over. The strokes of the pencil must always be made an equal distance apart, or the work will not be uniform, and a stroke must never be made across a line. Always turn the negative until, with a downward stroke, the mark may be filled in. The negative now receives the necessary spotting, *i. e.*, removing all transparent spots in the film, from whatever cause produced, by filling the spot with neutral tint (dry cake) color, ground to match the negative, and applied with a very finely pointed sable

brush ; though in the case of small pinholes, proceeding either from chemical causes or from dust
in the silver bath, or deposited in any way upon
the surface of the film previous to developing—at
least, upon a thin negative, and providing they
are not on the face—we recommend them to be
left untouched, as the small, black spot produced
in the resulting print is barely visible to the
naked eye, whereas it is impossible to put on a
touch of color, however minute, without its showing more or less ; it is then coated upon the back
with matt varnish, and the lights put in as they
occur with a fine leather or paper stump charged
with plumbago, or more effectually with the soft
crayons sold in round boxes for crayon drawing,
using the lighter green, flesh and gray shades,
softening the work with a stump after the effect
is produced.   In some negatives it will be more
convenient to work the chin and frontal depressions solely by dotting with the point of the pencil.   This, however, is only in cases where ladies
have a rather coarse skin.

Another Method.

A method much employed by English retouchers consists in first filling in all the imperfections completely; that is to say, the pencil is worked over the spots, etc., until no sign of them is visible. The inequalities of light and modelling are then done by short, straight lines running in a downward direction across the muscles and lines. The only parts of this process which are analogous to the last mentioned are the touching upon the nose and the frontal depression. Although the lines or strokes of the pencil take a downward direction, they are seldom parallel, and not equidistant from each other. By some retouchers the lines are made so fine as to give the appearance of dotting. The effect, however, is by no means so good as the lines.

A method was described in *The British Journal of Photography* of December 13, 1873, by Mr. G. Croughton, which we take the liberty of quoting for the benefit of those who do not hap-

pen to have seen the article referred to, as by it
a very effective picture is produced, and the method is a much quicker one than that described
above:

" In elderly people the lines and texture of the
face are far too marked in the enlarged negative ;
these can be much softened and reduced by printing through tracing paper. Strain the tracing
paper over the face of the negative, so interposing
a thickness of tracing paper between the sensi-
tized paper and the negative. I always strain
tracing paper on the reverse side of the negative,
as it serves to soften the printing, and is a capital
medium for working upon with the pencil to
strengthen the high lights. I can also, when
wanted, deepen the shadows of drapery, and I
make a varnish of Canada balsam, one dram ;
benzole, one ounce. Dipping a brush into this, I
run over the shades I want to deepen upon the
tracing paper ; the Canada balsam making the
paper more transparent in those parts, the light
acts more quickly and a greater depth of shadow

upon the print is the result, the distance the paper is from the film softening the edges. One plan I have adopted appears to me to be of great value for improving pictures which are flat from over-exposure or bad lighting, particularly if you wish your print to appear as if it were worked upon. The large head of a lady was done in this way, and the result, although there is not a touch upon the print, is such that more than one person has been tempted to bet that it was worked upon, and have only been convinced by a liberal use of sponge and water.

" The transparency was enlarged from a *carte*-sized negative to 10 x 8, varnished with Hughes's matt varnish, to which I had added a little gum elemi (this must be allowed at least twelve hours to dry); then with a mixture of putty powder and powdered blacklead I rubbed all over the face till I had what appeared to be an even, delicate tint throughout. I then cleared out the high lights with a piece of bread moulded to a point by the fingers."

The Americans seem to have adopted all the various methods. As a rule, however, they work rather more in a scumbling style, giving the strokes no particular direction, but making a touch wherever taste suggests or an inequality requires it; and this is the most convenient manner, no particular notice being taken of the direction of the lines of the skin. At the same time the work is done rather more systematically than the method we describe as scumbling. The touch might be called a saw-tooth one, such being the shape or character of the markings when examined by a powerful glass. They are made excessively fine, and produce a very charming effect of stipple when printed. This may be seen by examining many of the American portraits.

The methods in use upon the Continent of Europe are, perhaps, nearer the perfection of retouching than most of those generally employed; and, although different styles may be used in the same town or studio by various operators, they seem to get the desired artistic effect to greater perfection

than is done elsewhere. Continental negatives
are manifestly much over-worked in many instances ; but, as a rule, they please the public and
. the majority of photographers.

Herr Mohr, of Frankfort-on-the-Main, was, we
believe, the first to introduce negative retouching
into England.   True, there were a few who worked it secretly before his advent, but they guarded
their operations so carefully as to leave the rest
of the profession in ignorance as to the method
they employed for producing such good results ;
and until Herr Mohr taught it, it was not generally practiced to a very great extent.

We shall describe as nearly as possible the way
in which the negatives the author saw retouched
in different places upon the Continent were done.
In Germany the finished result resembles more
the hatching upon a crayon drawing or water col-
or.   The retoucher first proceeds to fill up all
transparent spots or lines, as in the aforemention-
ed methods, but in a little different manner, using
the point of the pencil more, lightly dotting until

all the markings—such as freckles, blotches, and optical exaggerations—are removed, and the face presents a tolerably even and smooth appearance, showing no signs of the blemishes. He now begins by means of cross hatching to model the face, placing a line or touch here and there as his eye happens to catch some unfinished portion wanting in gradation. The lights are put in their respective places, and gradually softened into the half-tones and shadows until the negative appears of that rotundity and modulation which a good retoucher so loves to see building up under his pencil. As he attains more experience he ventures upon bold touches, which give the negative much greater value and disperse the mechanical stiffness which beginners are too apt to give their touching. When the requisite amount of hatching is done (the lines of which are not at an angle of 45 deg. but about 30 deg.) our retoucher begins to fill in between the lines or cross hatches.

The method practiced by the French generally has the advantage over the German of being less liable to lose the likeness, although there is really a very trifling difference in the handling; in truth, in most of the methods the commencement is nearly the same, the negative being first made even throughout and then worked up until sufficiently soft. Most of the French retouchers, after having levelled the face and removed the inequalities, do the modelling required by making very fine, long, downward strokes, rather curved. This does not produce exactly the stipple most suitable, but makes the face very smooth and soft. The negatives are usually treated with gum or a mixture of gum and dextrine dissolved in warm water; this takes the pencil as readily as paper, but has the disadvantage of the film splitting, owing to the absorption of moisture by the gum and dextrine. The Germans retouch, as a rule, upon the varnish, using as a medium some gum solution which will give a bite to the pencil.

While treating this subject, we shall say a few words respecting our own retouching medium. Disclaiming totally the idea of using the book for advertising purposes, we still feel justified in introducing the subject, being convinced that by the use of a proper article results may be obtained quite unapproachable where varnish is used. The use of ordinary gum is attended with many disadvantages, as we have before mentioned. The films treated with it are very liable to split and crack if not varnished immediately, or if the varnish be applied cold, from the fact that they absorb moisture, which, if not thoroughly expelled, destroys the film. The medium mentioned has not this objection, being made with a view of overcoming the difficulty spoken of. Besides this, it renders the film very tough and gives a fine tooth, upon which a pencil of any grade may be used with as much ease as upon paper. This cannot be done upon varnished films.

When working upon mediums of any kind, breathing upon the plate must be avoided, as by so doing the film becomes softened and the pencil cuts through. The spotting is much easier upon films than upon the glazed varnish, and be-

sides which the touching is protected by subsequent varnishing.

This medium, though hundreds of bottles were
readily disposed of in England, has not been put
into the American market, for the author has few
opportunities of advertising competitively with
other preparations. Persons who find the various
methods described of use, and the book generally
of value, and who feel inclined to try this prepara-
tion upon the writer's assurance that it is the best
article for the purpose, may have any quantity
specially prepared for them by application to
Messrs. Anthony & Co.; also the matt varnish
mentioned, both of which preparations the author
always uses, keeping a small stock on hand.

The following solutions are employed by some
of the best retouchers, and have been highly recommended at different times, each being advo-
cated by the artist in whose hands it worked satisfactorily :

The first and, perhaps, the best kind of medium
intended to be used upon the varnished negative

is to dissolve eighty grains of gum Thus (white pine turpentine) in one ounce of benzole. When dissolved and filtered the solution is applied to the part to be worked upon with a tuft of cotton-wool. When it is nearly dry—which should be almost immediately after being applied—it may be rubbed gently with the ball of the finger. Retouching which at first is not satisfactorily done may be removed with a little benzole and the negative re-worked.

Another solution to be used in the same manner as above: Dissolve in one ounce of benzole, ten grains of clear resin ; allow to stand for a day or two before using.

Another :

Turpentine, . . .	1 ounce.
Gum dammar, . . .	10 grains.
Canada balsam, . . .	5 "

Another :

Spirits of turpentine, . .	3 ounces.
Cuttle-fish powder, . .	1 ounce.

This is strongly recommended by Mr. Beattie.

The directions for its use are the same as the above, the part being rubbed with the ball of the finger if streaks appear.

Another (to be applied cold to a negative which has been coated with gum water):

Ether, ...	15 ounces.
Sandarac, . . .	1 dram.
Shellac, ...	6 drams.
Mastic, ...	6 "

Dissolve, and add two and a half ounces of benzole.

One other method described—being a French idea, and both novel and efficacious—is to make a solution of—

Gum arabic, . . .	1 part.
Water, ...	7 parts.

And another, of—

Bichromate of potash, . .	3 parts.
Water, ...	7 "

The bichromate solution is added to the gum solution until it assumes the color of dark sherry wine. In this state it must be kept in the dark. The plates are then coated and kept in the dark until dry, when they are exposed for half an hour to strong light. They are then varnished with a hard matt varnish.

We can scarcely see the advantage of varnishing with the matt varnish before retouching, as the gum and bichromate would form hard, insoluble varnish themselves when exposed to light. Still, we give the quotation as we have it; the reader may try both systems and choose the one more suitable.

Besides the above, there are negative retouching varnishes made by some of the photographic dealers upon which the retouching is done without any medium or abrading substance being necessary. In using a varnish of this kind it should always be well tested to see that it does not crack or become tacky when heated or placed in the sun.

There is no better method beside retouching

upon mediumized films, than using a hard shellac varnish, and rubbing over the solution of resin in turpentine, mentioned in the chapter on Materials.

When negatives are retouched upon the gummed film, and prints taken from them before varnishing, there often appears, after varnishing, a number of minute yellow or brown spots; this is either caused by the paper being laid on while still damp or because the film has absorbed moisture and taken silver from the paper, which prints or darkens in the light. Care should, therefore, be taken to have both surfaces quite dry; and as a greater precaution, kaolin finely powdered may be dusted lightly over the film previous to the paper being placed in contact.

Retouching with a brush and color has been recommended, and is practiced by some retouchers here and abroad. When this is done (which takes much longer than with pencil) a very fine, stiff brush and *neutral tint* color is used. No gum must be mixed with the color, as it would adhere to the paper and spoil the negative.

Retouching with a needle point has also been mentioned, but we have never seen any very satisfactory results produced by it. If it be done, the parts intended to be lightened must be carefully scratched with the needle, keeping the negative warm while working—the object of this is to prevent ragged lines—and black lead brushed over to fill in the scratches so produced. When all the shadows have been so worked, the too strong lights are lightened by scratching, no lead being, of course, used. The negative, when varnished, is then ready for the printer. For this process a special collodion is necessary. A little fine resin or gum added to an ordinary collodion will answer the same purpose ; the negative, after washing, has a weak solution of albumen—strength. one ounce to twenty ounces of water—flowed over it and allowed to dry. By using a thin collodion and keeping the plate warm the scratching can be done with much greater facility. The only advantage we can see in such a process is where very hard, over-dense negatives are to be worked, in which case the over-dense portions are made much lighter by the scratching process.

Before concluding this chapter, a few words about the retouching machines that have been advertised within the past few months may not be out of place. To every sensible man it must be patent that no artistic pursuits can be carried on by any mechanical arrangement, however ingeniously planned. And without wishing to say anything derogatory to either of the machines advertised, the author feels it a duty, in writing a book of this kind, to avoid misleading the reader, and to point out any practice likely to embarrass a beginner. As mechanical contrivances these machines have each their respective merits, but with all of them the same amount of talent is required to guide them as to guide a pencil; and this when coupled with the practice necessary to become accustomed to the use of these machines, to prevent them either from spoiling a negative or doing too much upon it, leave little in favor of machinery as a retouching aid.

Besides, the best of these machines are not applicable to any of the methods described in this book, and in using them no guidance could be had from the foregoing chapters further than the modelling is concerned. These remarks apply to studies of heads in all kinds of work, in whatsoever material executed.

CHAPTER V.

Rembrandts, Landscapes, etc.

REMBRANDTS.

THIS kind of portraiture will be found more difficult to manage. As a rule, photographers who attempt this style of lighting either make the light upon the profile too strong or the shadow too deep. One fault is quite as troublesome to the retoucher as the other. It is to be regretted that photographers do not content themselves with soft effects produced by the first development, and not resort to after-intensification. thereby destroying all the detail in the light side of the face.

However dense a light may be in nature, it always contains detail and modulation, and so it should be in a negative. Commencing with the edge of the light upon the forehead—assuming the negative to be profile, or nearly so, as Rembrandts usually are—soften the light into the surrounding parts until the temporal arch or crest is reached ; in this case the arch should receive (comparatively with parts around it) more light and show more plainly, although in shade, than if the negative were an ordinarily lighted one, taking care to preserve relative importance of detail and careful handling of reflexes. The malar bone and the palpabral muscles should all contain a little more prominence than in plainly lighted negatives. We do not mean that they must be whiter ; but the modelling, in order to show well when printed as deeply as it is necessary to print Rembrandts, must be made to contain more contrast.

The light on the nose must be carefully worked out, and also the corner of the eyes ; the deep shadow formed by the orbitar arch in under-exposed negatives will require a great deal of working to make it print properly. Much of this may be stopped out at the back of the negative, as also much of the shadow side, if too thin. Of course, this must be done after the retouching has been carried as far as it is possible. Upon thin negatives it is sometimes a difficult matter to get the pencil to take where it has already gone over; that is, if sufficient density be not obtained by the first application of the pencil, it is not easy to make the second application take. In such cases, by using the matt varnish at the back, and working upon it, sufficient density may be secured. The eyes in a Rembrandt negative will require no working if the head be profile, or nearly so, as they are at first generally too strongly lighted, unless the negative be particularly well lighted; they are, therefore, left to be retouched in the print.

A pleasing effect may be produced—when not supplied in the background—by lightening it close to the figure or face upon one side and some distance from it on the other.

LANDSCAPES.

For landscapes a great degree of skill is not required. The sky is usually the principal part to be worked upon; for this purpose it is only necessary to work in a cloud effect suitable to the subject with ivory black upon the back of the negative. Any deep shadows, that may suggest themselves as being too dense to the retoucher, may be treated with plumbago, and the landscape itself should be masked while the clouds are being printed. This mask may be placed upon the glass of the printing-frame, and should be cut large enough to overlap the outline a quarter of an inch. When the sky is just dark enough to show the clouds clearly—though not as dark, of course, as they are to be when finished—the mask is removed and the rest of the picture printed in.

When it is required to print a natural sky in by combination printing, the simplest method we have found to answer in practice is to make two masks a shade larger than the parts they are to protect

—one to cover the sky and the other the landscape portion of the negative. These are placed upon the back of the negatives, and a combination print of the two made by first exposing the sensitive paper under the cloud negative and then adjusting it to the landscape negative, the sky of which is also masked. The masks having both been on the backs of the negatives, the line between sky and landscape will not be visible unless the prints were made in too strong a light. The paper is then removed. When combination prints of clouds are made, the two printings must manifestly be carried on in the same light, otherwise they would be different in tone.

Frequently the lines in landscapes are not nicely balanced; for instance, a mountain may be shown in the distance on one side, and nothing to counterbalance it on the other side of the picture. When this occurs, by judiciously distributing some clouds on the side opposite the offending mountain, the effect may often be subdued; lightening the sky above the mountain will also assist in this.

Printing Clean Ground in Large Portraits.

It often happens that a large negative, which is perfect in other respects, has a very streaky and dirty background. To print from such negatives as they are, only reflects discredit upon the photographer. Vignettes are not wished for, and combination printing is very troublesome. By following the under-mentioned directions, prints with perfectly clean grounds may be made from this class of negatives with but little trouble :

First trace the outline of the figure upon paper and lay the paper upon a thick piece of felt, such as is used for printing-frame pads ; cut through with a sharp knife both paper and pad. We now have a felt pad exactly the size of the figure. Place bits of cork at the upper corners and edges of the negative –upon the background half only. Now lay the silvered paper upon the negative, fastening the corners to strain the paper pretty tightly. Next lay the felt mask upon the paper just over the figure and close the frame. The ob-

ject of this is to cause the felt pad to press th*
paper into close contact with the figure, while the
corks keep the paper some distance from the negative on the background, thus printing the figure
sharply but throwing the background so much out
of focus that the light diffuses and produces a
perfectly even ground. This "dodge" in the case
of copies is invaluable. It will scarcely pay to
use felt for one copy—several thicknesses of blot-
ting-paper may be substituted for single prints
—but for a number of copies the felt is better.

Cracks in Films.

If not too wide, cracks in films may be easily
removed by rubbing in with the ball of the finger
either lampblack, indigo, or plumbago, selecting
whichever of the three will more nearly match the
printing density of that part of the negative, so as
to avoid printing a white line. Soft French pas-
tels are very useful for this purpose. The grays
can be had in tones to correspond precisely with
any kind of negative. It is only necessary to rub

che finger charged with pastel across the lines or cracks.

The crayon sauces supersede all others for this purpose. Of course, large cracks will have to be touched out with color, and as color will not take kindly upon bare glass it will be found necessary to varnish the negative beforehand.

CHAPTER VI.

Enamelling Prints, Intensification of Negatives, etc.

ENAMELLING PRINTS.

THIS fashion, which for a time bade fair to gain favor with the profession, is gradually losing its charm. A *good* picture requires no such superfluous finish to add to its beauty; while, on the other hand, if the picture be finished in an indifferent manner, the enamelling suggests the idea that such means had been resorted to for the purpose of hiding some of the imperfections in a glaring polish, which would have the effect of subduing by its attractive appearance the minor defects. There are, however, many persons who are admirers of the finish, and many whose customers prefer it to ordinary albumen paper finish. For the benefit of such we describe the methods of enamelling we have employed, and which will be found to produce very good and, at the same time, very brilliant results.

The following will be useful in affording the toughest film, although a little more troublesome than those methods usually practiced : The first process, after the finished prints have left the water, is to lay them in warm water until they are required for use. Have a solution of gelatine, made by dissolving one ounce of gelatine in half a pint of water. To effect this, allow the gelatine to remain in the cold water until well swollen ; pour off the cold and then warm gently and add one dram of white sugar. When dissolved pour the gelatine into a clean dish, and, taking the prints from the warm water, blot them and lay them upon the solution of gelatine in the same manner as floating albumenized paper upon a silver bath. Allow to remain a few seconds, and lay them upon their backs on clean paper to dry.

The plates are now prepared by polishing first with a solution of white wax in benzole in the proportion of five grains to the ounce of benzole. A little of the solution is poured upon the glass and spread over with a piece of rag, and finally polished with a clean tuft of cotton-wool. When all are waxed, collodionize with plain collodion, and place when set, in cold water until all greasy lines have disappeared. The prints have now to be laid upon the glass. To do this they must first be placed in a solution of chrome alum two per cent. strength, about 90 deg. Fah., and then placed upon the glass with a piece of waxed paper over them. Before they are quite dry, paste a piece of stout cartridge paper at their backs. Stroke out the water and allow them to dry, when, if properly done, they will spring from the glass. They may now be cut to the required sizes, and, if medallions, embossed in the cameo press. By using this method, the collodion, from

being placed in water immediately, is less liable
to catch particles of dust that may be flying.

Another method is to prepare the glasses as
above, collodionize, and allow to dry. When dry,
run a line of solution of india-rubber around the
edges to prevent the film from leaving them. The
prints are then floated upon the gelatine solution
and placed immediately upon the glass. The
water and superfluous gelatine is stroked out, care
being taken that there are no minute air-bells between the print and the collodion, and the prints
backed with paper and allowed to dry. This is
the simplest method, but not quite so neat nor
so sure as the first mentioned. The gelatine may
be swilled over the plate and the wet print laid
down upon it with a little better result, ensuring
greater immunity from air-bells.

By laying albumen prints immediately after
they are taken from the washing water upon
plates collodionized and soaked in water as described, a very good enamelled surface may be
secured.

Attempts have been made to produce the fine enamelled surface with a varnish; but the results are far from being satisfactory, and the process is quite as, if not more, troublesome.

One drawback to enamelling is the great difficulty of spotting the prints. Water color washes away or runs when the gelatine is put on, and oil colors do not meet the requirements of the case. By using a quantity of gum with the color and waxing the prints, after spotting, they can be made to match tolerably well. Colors are also supplied to retouch the prints before they are glazed; but we cannot give an opinion as to their efficacy, not having used them ourselves. By mixing the colors used with albumen they do not run so much, as the albumen coagulates when in contact with the warm gelatine; but, even then, the color lies unevenly and granularly. A drop of solution of gum dammar in ether will fix the touching; or the whole print, if much worked upon, may be brushed over with matt varnish. Small spots may be obliterated with a soft pencil.

CHEMICAL INTENSIFICATION OF PARTS OF
NEGATIVES.

It often happens that a negative could be made perfect if it were possible to give intensity to certain parts only. A landscape, for instance, may have a finely clouded sky, but the view portion be too weak for printing; if it were intensified the sky would be lost. Proceed by making ready a solution of iodide of potassium and iodine about the color of dark sherry. To prepare this solution add iodine to water until a dark, muddy precipitate is formed; then add iodide of potassium until the liquid clears, and dilute with water to the required strength. Having developed the negative, wash well and flood with the iodine solution, and rinse with clean water. Allow it to dry, and run a line of varnish around the edge to prevent the film leaving the glass during the second development.

When thoroughly dry go round the edges of the part to be intensified with a large brush (finely pointed) charged with water   This line must, of course, be made inside the contour line ; keep it well flooded until the contour is all drawn, and with a larger brush fill in the space to be strengthened with water.   This will have to be done very skillfully or the lines of the brush will show. When the part is well covered with water pour on the intensifier, which will flow over the wet portion only, stopping at the edges where they come in contact with the dry part of the film. When the intensifier has done its work wash again, fix and dry, when the negative will be properly intensified in all parts.   This process may be employed to intensify a face, drapery, or backgrounds; or, by substituting cyanide of potassium for the intensifier, the parts may be reduced if too strong.   At first sight it would appear that the contour line would be sharp, or cut out, as it were ; this, however, does not happen if skillfully managed, as the extreme edge dries slowly during the painting, thus softening that which would otherwise appear too strong.

A varnish composed of gum anime in benzole,
colored with iodine, may be applied to backs of
negatives, and when dry removed from all light
portions with benzole or alcohol with very good
results.   Hard landscapes may in this way be
very evenly printed.

SPOTTING PRINTS.

When the negatives are properly retouched
and have no specks of dirt or chemical stains upon
them the proofs will, provided they were carefully
printed, require no spotting ; but if the negatives
were carelessly taken, badly spotted or retouched,
a white spot upon the print will occur wherever
a dark one exists in the negative.

For spotting these mix upon a palette a color
to match as nearly possible the tone of the print.
Black, brown, rose madder, and neutral tint in
proper proportion will match any photographic
tone nearly enough for general work.   A little
gum must be ground with the color to make it
run more freely, and to give it the same glaze as

the albumenized paper. Use a small, finely-pointed red sable brush charged with color, taking only sufficient to cover the defect. Too much color in the brush is not advisable. being more difficult to work with and often making the spots too dark. It is always better to have the touching a little lighter inst ' of a shade darker than the photograph. The photographs, when touched, will be much improved if polished with the following paste :

Encaustic Paste Formula.—Dissolve with gentle heat—

White wax (pure), . . 3 ounces.
Essence of turpentine (white), 3½ "
Copal varnish (pure), . . 1½ dram.
Oil of lavender, . . ½ "

Rub a little of the paste over the picture with a soft rag, and polish with a piece of old, soft flannel.

The lighter specks in the face may be worked out delicately with a hard pencil. Prints to be burnished should be spotted rather lightly, as the touching will usually show darker when finished.

www.ingramcontent.com/pod-product-compliance
Lightning Source LLC
Chambersburg PA
CBHW031440280326
41927CB00038B/1386